Fish Discover Water Last

Richard L. Grossman

on corporations, democracy and us

Edited by Anna Gyorgy

Fish Discover Water Last

"It is sometimes said that 'fish discover water last.' And I think that applies to us. We've been colonized. We're a colonized people. We've lived in a corporate culture for the last hundred years. We're surrounded by the icons, and images and propaganda, and how many hundreds of millions of dollars of constant advertising. It's affected our ability to think. We censor ourselves all the time. We censor our goals. We censor our tactics and strategies. We don't demand what we know we want and what we need. And that's what we need to begin changing."

From *Defining the Corporation, Defining Ourselves*, Richard Grossman's talk at the University of Colorado, Boulder, February 1997

This work is dedicated to Alyssa Grossman,
her sons, and the many people
who remember and miss her father.

Published by Human Error Publishing
www.humanerrorpublishing.com
paul@humanerrorpublishing.com

ISBN#: 978-1-948521-44-4

Cover design
Font cover graphic: "Spawning Salmon" by Cynthia Fisher,
courtesy of the artist. *www.bigbangmosaics.com*

Back cover: Portrait by Robert Shetterly, courtesy of the
artist. *https://www.americanswhotellthetruth.org/por-
traits/richard-grossman*

Editor's Note

The sudden passing of Richard Lee Grossman in November 2011 at age 68 was a tragic shock for family and friends. It also left a vacuum in the highly charged U.S. political scene of the time with its active Occupy movement, more attuned to fundamental aspects of his analysis.

An acknowledged expert on the Constitution, law and democracy, citizens' rights and the lack of them, Richard Grossman called for a study of U.S. history to understand why rights are denied in this country. He did so with wit and passion, encouraging others.

His work combined decades of research and practice, teaching and organizing, with clarity and criticism, humor and great love and appreciation for the natural world.

Before melanoma claimed him, he was preparing a new book, his "Magnum Opus," with accompanying booklet. Sadly, this major work remains unwritten. However the productive 'earthling,' a favorite term, left behind a wealth of material and thought in his books, lectures and interviews, critical letters, well-crafted opinion pieces -- and draft legislation. Many of these are scattered around the internet, some collected and offered with special care (see Appendix).

Taken together, they show the development of Richard Grossman's thought and work. These led to strategic projects pursued into his last months and weeks, as he worked with local and statewide groups in his home state of New York on a law and movement to criminalize hydraulic fracturing, or 'fracking,' for natural gas. As well as drafting legislation to ban corporations entirely.

Many of Richard Grossman's writings are available in print or online. But his public oratory is so distinctive, that here

I present mainly excerpts from talks and interviews given from 1995 to 2011, most still available online. The quotes are woven to narrate key points in his analysis, with sources given in footnotes.

It is said, he tells us, that "fish discover water last." Likewise we, who live in a corporate empire state, may not be aware of the system in which we all 'swim,' with its encompassing structure set in law and "clothed in the Constitution." And its broad grip on popular culture and lore.

Since Richard Grossman's passing, the extent and disastrous results of corporate control of government and society have become ever more apparent, and the need for action and change ever more urgent. We don't know what Richard Grossman would be saying were he alive now, but shortly after his death a friend of his said Richard's thought and analysis was so ahead of his time, it would take 20 years to be understood and fully appreciated.

Thus we hope that this small volume, looking back on his years of reflection and work in his own words, will be understood and appreciated in this decade, and beyond.

And that his thoughts and conclusions can contribute to the new movements for justice happening on many levels.

Anna Gyorgy, Wendell, Massachusetts

Table of Contents

"Fish Discover Water Last":

Background

Richard Grossman opened his November 2006 speech, "When Injustice is Legal," at Antioch College in Yellow Springs, Ohio, saying:

In 1972 the English historian Christopher Hill wrote something about history I'd like to read:

> *History has to be rewritten in every generation. Although the past does not change, the present does. Each new generation asks new questions of the past. And finds new areas of sympathy as it relives different aspects of the experiences of its predecessors.*
>
> *Most of our history is written about, and from the point of view of, a very tiny fragment of the population. Each generation, to put it another way, rescues new areas from what its predecessors arrogantly and snobbishly dismissed as the 'lunatic fringe.'*

So I'm very happy to be part of that 'lunatic fringe' of my generation.[1]

I came to Washington, D.C. in 1976 from California, where I'd spent the previous three years working on the first statewide antinuclear referendum, Proposition 15, on the ballot in June of 1976.

I spent ten years with the group Environmentalists for Full Employment, doing some work on nature and labor, and work and the environment, trying to build some bridges there, and looking at data about jobs vs the environment...

I spent a little bit of time at Greenpeace. After that, I was a guest fellow at the Institute for Policy Studies in Washington, D.C. And then I spent two years working with the Highlander

Center in Tennessee, which was in the forefront of the grassroots anti-toxics movement. And we developed something called STP Schools, for Stop the Poisoning...

I also started publishing a little rag called "The Wrenching Debate Gazette" to begin some of the conversation we're talking about here.

Because I had had sort of an epiphany in 1988 or so. I said: "I've done enough data. We have enough data, we know the data, we don't need any more 'data.' What we need is action, we need commensurate action." And I didn't know where I thought that action should go.[2]

I had concluded that this country needed significant transitions, in investment and production, manufacturing, work and consumption. That from an ecological, workers' rights and equity standpoint, the data were pretty overwhelming.

Although millions of people had formed thousands of civic, activist and issue groups, and had been courageously and valiantly organizing, mobilizing, passing laws, filing lawsuits, marching, writing books and tracts, and going to jail and doing civil disobedience: the work hadn't been adding up.

So much of the organizing seemed to be single issue defense. One issue at a time, basically defensive: trying to stop some stupid idea, some destructive investment or production system. And over and over again. With very little spilling out across issue, across constituency lines.

I decided I wasn't going to do single issue defense any more, and began to explore. Saying: "Well, I'll start looking at why it is so hard in this country, even when majority sentiment seems to be going in a certain way, to bring about fundamental change."[3]

Fortuitously, but somewhat logically, I chose the corporation as my point of entry. Logically, because it was the dominant institution of our era, and has been for the last 100 years. And we lucked out. Because we found that it leads us into everything: back to the nation's founding, back to the Constitution. It's about law, it opens up to peoples' movements, in the context of rights.[4]

I. "How did we get into this mess?"

Corporate roots

Richard Grossman spoke at the May 1996 Global Teach-in 2 of the International Forum on Globalization. Founded in 1994, the IFG brought together leading activists and researchers from the North and Global South to investigate and critique corporate globalization. Here are excerpts from his presentation, recorded by Maria Gilardin for TUC Radio.

Democracy and the Historical Relationship Between Citizens and Corporations

In the year 1407, the good sovereign king Henry IV of England chartered the Company of Merchants and Adventurers, the ancestor of the East India Company. Granting it monopoly control over exports of certain manufacturers. The empire started to expand, wealth began to flow into England.

In 1553, the Crown chartered the Russian Company, granting monopoly privilege over certain trade routes to Russia. The company also got special concessions from the Tzar.

In 1553, the Africa Company was chartered and given special privileges to pursue the slave trade.

In 1557 the Spanish Company was chartered, given special privileges and monopolies to control the wine and olive oil trade with Spain and Portugal.

In 1578 the Eastland Company was created, given sole privilege to carry on trade with Scandinavian countries. It was also granted additional authority to make laws, impose fines, and imprison people.

In 1581 the Levant Company was created, to trade with Turkey. In 1592 this company merged with the Turkey Company and the Venice Company, in which Queen Elizabeth was a shareholder, to form the East India Company.

In 1605 the East India Company was given a charter in perpetuity. And given exclusive rights to trade in specified areas of Europe, East and West Asia, North and West Africa.

What was the purpose of these and other global corporations of those days? These chips off the old block of sovereignty?

Well, in hindsight we can be very clear, that their mission was to buy cheap, to sell dear, to limit or prevent competition, to vacuum out resources, to display fierce violence, and to perpetuate violence to people, species and places. To destroy existing cultures and social relationships. To replace independence with dependence, to eradicate peoples' sense of their own histories. To get people to incorporate the corporation's values, myths and world views.

To create a class of bureaucrats and civil servants to serve their needs. To define people as subjects, objects, property, invisible and anything else they wanted to define them as.

To control all dispute resolution, to raise armies and navies and wage war. To write laws, including laws and doctrines which legalize and institutionalize the corporation's destructive and dominating acts.

To enforce laws, to impose punishments, including executions. In other words, to govern. And to govern dictatorially, but with guile.

From these hundreds of years of experiences, can't we deduce the nature of the corporate fiction? These corporations didn't just create some excessive harms.

They didn't just occasionally exploit. They didn't just drive bargains. They were, by definition, by their nature, oppressors.

It's an old story, isn't it? The cults of the few tyrannizing the many.

And the many. What about them? Who were they?

They were the violated and the dehumanized, the oppressed. The people blocked from being and acting fully human, from participating in their own governance. From defining their own lives, their own work, their own values.

Today the majority of the people in the world are oppressed by the few. And the oppressive vehicle of choice is -- guess what? The global corporation.

So isn't it time that we started acting like oppressed people? *(laughter, applause)*

Well the question is, what kind of oppressed people? The conscious oppressed people? Or the unconscious oppressed people?

Here are some characteristics of the unconscious oppressed people, which I've stolen from Paolo Freire:

> *They believe that the oppressor is the model of humanity. They adopt the oppressor's values. They aspire to be like the most eminent and respectable of the oppressors. They are drawn by the irresistible attraction to the oppressor's way of life, thereby modeling their civil, educational and other institutions after the oppressor's institutions. They accept the dominance and authority of the oppressors as just and appropriate, or as inevitable.*

They concede to the oppressor basic legal and cultural authority, to define investment, production and work. And to define values and concepts, such as: progress, efficiency, productivity, sustainability, legal violence, justice, freedom, human rights, liberty, nature, security, property, prosperity, peace, public, private and personhood.

They allow, even encourage, oppressors to educate and entertain their children. They fear governing themselves. They fear to define their own societies. They do not know their own history. They think and talk and strategize in the language of the oppressors. They pursue their grievances only in the dens of the oppressors. They confuse freedom with the maintenance of the status quo.

And what about the conscious oppressed? Well,

they are people in the process of moving, of uncovering their own histories, especially by examining events and eras glorified and distorted by the oppressors. They are relearning their languages and their culture. They are realizing how naive they have been.

They are coming to see their oppression as a distortion of being fully human. That to permit themselves to be treated as objects, as property, as subjects, as invisible, to permit one's community to be treated as a fiefdom, is nuts. Who are joining to help each other to stop regarding the oppressors as abstract forces, as created by God or Mother Nature. Who are confronting their realities analytically, teaching themselves by investigations and intentional discussions and authentic action, not merely to curb the worst excesses of the oppressors, but to craft resistance which is about taking power and legitimacy from the oppressors. And by assuming the authority to govern themselves.

Who see freedom not just as a gift, or an endowment, but as a process by which they can aspire to create institutions of self-governance, and that they can maintain these institutions by acting responsibly and accountably to one another. Who are impatient, and also patient.

That's the kind of oppressed people that we need to be, and I think as a result of the efforts and struggles versus tyranny, and for consciousness, of people around the globe, across the centuries and centuries and in recent times, that that's the people we're becoming.

In Freire's words: "We're moving towards the historical processes as responsible subjects, not as objects, who can work with each other. Not to grovel for concessions, or fawn over the false generosity of the oppressors, but to transform our world."

So what does this mean for us today? Well, we have some models that we can use as guides. The triumph of the majority of the people in South Africa. The triumph of the Indian people, in India. Our own American Revolution.

But for each of these events and processes, it's important that we look to see what happened and what didn't happen, to reexamine the history. [5]

II. From Revolution to Corporate Empire State

The American Revolution, what was it?

One of the things it was: it replaced a dictatorial oppressor with a very different idea, the idea of self-governance. And it sent the idea of the monarchy packing.

It also transformed dictatorial crown corporations, like the Massachusetts colony, the Virginia colony, and the Carolina colony, into constitutionalized states.

What it was not: It was not self-governance and democracy for all.[6]

Go back and read the Constitution, and the laws of the states. In fact, 20 percent of the people at the time in North America denied the rights of 80 percent: not only African American slaves, but African Americans who weren't slaves, women, indentured servants, white men without property, native peoples, not to mention the fauna and flora and mountains and rivers.

They set up a slave system, or continued the slave system that had existed.

But what is a system? It's not just an isolated relationship between a master and a slave. It covered the entire country, and was a mechanism of ordering society and enabling slave masters to control the government.[7]

The word 'corporation' is not mentioned in the U.S. Constitution. And although the minority who recognized themselves as people instituted mechanisms to define and limit the corporation with precision, to keep it from political rights and power, by the end of the 19th century the corporation had waged a counterrevolution. It had transformed the laws, and was on its way to becoming -- to being -- what corporations had been revealed as for the previous 300 years.

With their wealth and power, they constitutionalized corporate rights over the decision-making of what counts. In other words, basic decision-making that shapes our lives and our communities, was declared beyond the authority of the people.

So that even when the excluded classes of people: the African Americans, native people, women, men without property, after a century of struggle had 'become people,' had won their rights, the corporate culture was powerful enough to transform all of us into consumers.

I go through this because it's vital, in our road to consciousness, and in our engaging in authentic action, to understand that what corporations are now doing around the world, they accomplished in the United States of America a hundred years ago.[8]

"When Injustice is Legal": learning from the Abolitionists

Among the tasks of the abolitionists was to help people see what was happening. To see what was in their midst. It is often said that 'fish discover water last.' They were living within this system.

The abolitionists set out in the early 1830s, at a time of increasing slave revolts and the underground railroad, when African Americans, free and slaved, were resisting, sometimes with violence.

They had an enormous job to do. And what has impressed me the most is that it took them thirty years to figure out what the problem was, to argue it out.[9]

They asked: "What's the problem here? Is it the racism and the cruelty and the excess? What do we want to solve?" And the answers were not self-evident. Because if they defined the problem as cruel masters, then they would work to make kinder masters. Maybe set up a Slave Protection Agency, like the EPA...

Instead they engaged in intense debates, discussions, arguments, and came to a very different perspective: that something was fundamentally wrong in the law of the land. In the Constitution itself.

Slavery was legal. The law enabled it. It made it possible.[10]

There are two parts in the Constitution that are very relevant. One is that if a bonded laborer, a slave or indentured servant ran away, and ran to a non-slave state, ran to the north, the government -- local, state or federal -- was required to return that slave to his or her master. So that the full force and might, the armed might of the nation, was to support the institution of slavery.[11]

Secondly, there was a clause in the Constitution that slaves would be counted as 3/5ths of a person. That meant that the slave states counted 3/5ths of a person for each slave and were appropriated more Congressional and electoral college representatives. Which meant that up until the Civil War, the slave states controlled the federal government.[12]

The abolitionists understood that slavery was a slave system around which the economy and much of the social relations of the country were built. Of the whole country, not just the South. Slavery was central to progress, jobs, wealth, the Good Life.

In that atmosphere, abolitionists began to talk about this stuff. Putting it into the language of rights and rights denied. Into the language of the ideals of the Revolution, of the Declaration of Independence.

And basically concluded that they could not envision achieving the goal of emancipation and equality, of a country without slavery, under the existing constitution, set of laws, and culture. So they set out to change that.[13]

The target of their work was not going to be the slave-masters. They didn't go around negotiating with slave-masters to be socially responsible or sign voluntary codes of conduct.

They said: "Our fight is not with the slavemasters, because we're going to put you off the earth. But our focus is in fact our public officials, our public servants, it's government."

And therefore the arena is the village square, and the arena is our legislature.

When the Civil War had destroyed the trappings and substance of the slavocracy in the South there was an opportunity to change the Constitution. So they drove the

Thirteenth and Fourteenth and Fifteenth Amendments into the Constitution of the United States. Because they were ready. They had thought about it. They knew what they needed to do.

And then you had a flourishing of an historical moment for a decade or so, with Reconstruction and the amendments and laws passed in Congress. Which some people call a Second American Revolution.

It was sort of the intermediate between the slave state and the rise of the corporate state. When people actually tried to build a democracy state, as some people had intended from the beginning. To be characterized by free labor, no wage slavery to replace chattel slavery.

And unfortunately that was crushed...[14]

Then you had the worst in irony, that the Fourteenth Amendment became a primary tool for the corporate class to clothe itself in the Constitution of the United States.[15]

I'm going to close with one last thing about the anti-slavery movement and abolition.

Because it's so parallel. Because you had a slave state, a creation of law. It did not exist on its own. It was a creation of law, just like the corporate state. And when people rose up to go against slavery, they did not go up against the slave owners. They went up against the slave state, against the Constitution.

That's why (abolitionist leader William Lloyd) Garrison, at public appearances would burn the Constitution, as a covenant with death and an agreement with hell. Because the fundamental constitutional and cultural roots of slavery were in the Constitution.

Theodore Weld, one of the great orators of the time, wrote a 1200 page book, "Slavery as it Is," detailing all the horrors and abuses of slavery. As soon as he wrote it, he said: "I will not talk about the treatment of slaves, because it detracts from going to the underpinnings." We can't talk about the abuses and the excesses, because it's about the under-pinnings.[16]

And only twenty years later, you get some judges on the Supreme Court taking the Fourteenth Amendment, and just wrapping it around the corporate class. Enabling them to wield the Constitution against us over a hundred years later.[17]

A hundred years of accumulated corporate state law. We had a hundred years of accumulated corporate state lore. They have rewritten our creation story, they have got it into our minds. They channel our thinking, our civic activism. They diminish our aspirations.

We don't talk about what we really want. We think about, "Oh, maybe this is the best we can do."[18]

What the Populists were all about: 1890 -1896

In 1890 there was the last citizen effort to challenge the corporate state. Urban workers, intellectuals and farmers coming together to form the Populist movement, in 1885 to the end of the century -- 1896.

People were very clear that they were suffering harms at the hands of corporations, that corporations had become the rulers. And so the slogan of all the Farmer's Parties and People's Parties was: "We have to end the corporate state."

They weren't talking about regulating the corporations to decrease the amount of harms they were doing. They weren't talking about legalizing poisoning. They were talking about ending the corporate state. And resurrecting the ideals of self-governance.[19]

They saw the corporate state coming out of the rise of the robber barons, the mixing of the Northern capitalists and the Southern ex-slavemasters.[20]

They understood that the corporation had turned the law and culture around, making property rights greater than human rights. And thus there could be no such thing as self-governance.[21]

The Populists were very clear. They said: "We don't accept as progress what the corporate state is bringing to us. We define progress in a very different way." [22]

For the past 100 years there has been no counterforce to the corporate class to challenge the corporate class authority to govern in this country. And if we look at the difference between the Populist movement and the Progressive Era, we can see that distinction very clearly.[23]

Progressives and the New Deal:
regulating harms -- and us

After the Populists were crushed at the end of the 1800s, we had a movement for the next 15 years or so called the Progressive Era. And we learn more about that in school than we learn about the Populists.

And I think it's very important, in the process of rethinking how we got here, into this mess, to see that the Progressives were almost the opposite of the Populists. In that they basically conceded that the corporation would be the dominant institution of our time, and that the best they could do would be to try to make it a little less bad. To try and find the best men to run it, and kind of control them around the edges.[24]

The whole so-called 'Progressive agenda' was a regulatory administrative law agenda. It was about accepting and embracing the realities that had been accomplished: the private ordering of economic decision-making.

That the corporate class would make the decisions over where they would invest our money; what technologies they would choose; how they would organize production and manufacturing; how they would organize work. How they would in fact wield the law of our state and of the nation against us. That was done by 1900.

The so-called misnamed 'Progressive Era' was all about setting up these regulatory administrative structures that would only be about dealing with the impacts, mitigating the impacts, lessening the abuses.

They did nothing to change the total victory over the law: the constitutionalizing of the business corporation; the tying of the hands of our municipal corporations, stripped of any governing authority, essentially concentrating governance in the hands of the corporate board and backing them with the law of the state and the law of the nation.

So that when we get to the New Deal, which was the epitome of the regulatory administrative state, with the Securities and Exchange Commission and the National Labor Relations Act, and the Comptroller of the Currency and all these regulatory bodies, the Food and Drug Administration, which came a little earlier, none of that provided any ability for people resisting particular wrongs to challenge that history. Because the business corporation had already been constitutionalized.[25]

And when the corporate lawyers, with the help of progressive leaders, began to set up the regulatory structure, they began to do that to channel us -- the source of all political power in this country, the sovereign people -- away from constitutional questions, from fundamental questions of rights, such as: who gets rights and who defines what? Who's in charge? Who gets to wield the law against whom? Who gets to wield the might of the nation against whom? Who gets to wield the Constitution against whom?

So during the New Deal and the Great Depression, it was the Progressive agenda that was picked up, not the Populist agenda.[26]

When you get into the regulatory agencies of the 1930s and '40s and '50s and then the environmental laws of the '60s and '70s and '80s on the federal and the state level, the business corporation had been wrapped in the Constitution.[27]

So we struggle to pass these regulatory laws, and have for a hundred years, and then we struggle to enforce them. And even if we win, what are we winning? What we're enforcing is a request, or a plea, that they cause a little less harm, invade a few less of our rights.[28]

III. Why we can't win with a stacked deck

For an explanation of how corporations were endowed by the courts over the years with the constitutional powers of the First, Fourth, Fifth and Fourteenth Amendments, see a draft legal brief "intended to assist communities organizing to challenge the United States government's gift of constitutional powers to property organized as corporations" by Richard L. Grossman, Thomas Linzey, Esq., and Daniel E. Brannen, Jr., Esq. © 2003 at http://www.ratical.org/corporations/demoBrief.html

See also: "When Corporations Wield the Constitution," by Richard L. Grossman and Ward Morehouse, November 2002 (https://ratical.org/corporations/WCWtC.html)

Corporations, because the corporation is a person, can in fact use a law enacted to protect the rights of freed slaves during Reconstruction to sue a community for loss of future profits if they get in the way of their siting a Walmart store, or a quarry, or a toxic dump, or an incinerator, or any other piece of crap that a community doesn't want. Loss of future profits plus attorneys' fees. You're talking about billions of dollars.

So when the town of Wellfleet in the 1990s initially said 'no' to a cell phone tower, the Omnipoint corporation came and said: "We're suing you under this Reconstruction Era law, and you're going to pay us future profits for the next 25 years for what we would have earned through those cell towers."

And so what does Wellfleet do?

Wellfleet then collapses, of course. It's the law, it's legal! When a community gets together to say: "We don't want this store, we don't want this incinerator, we don't want this factory farm," whatever it is, the first barrier they hit is the law of the land.

There are some wonderful words in the Supreme Court decision throwing Eugene Debs in jail in 1895. A unanimous decision by the Supreme Court, saying: "The entire strength of the nation may be used to enforce in any part of the land the full and free exercise of all national powers, and the security of all rights entrusted by the Constitution to its care. If the emergency arises, the army of the nation and all its militia are at the service of the nation to compel obedience to its laws."[29]

That's pretty stirring language. When did we ever have that kind of language for the rabble, for the denied? There was no language like that in even Brown vs. Board of Education. Nothing stirring like that. "With all slow speed," or whatever they said.... Among the points I'm trying to make is that the rabble, the majority, never had control in this country.[30]

Except for some blips in this century, we've been playing in their ballpark, under their rules, within what has become the equivalent of the monarchy culture, which I think is a corporate colonial culture.

They've gotten our language. They've taken our minds. I think they've taken our ability, to a large extent, to strategize. They've affected how we think. And how we talk to one another.[31]

We need to look at what's going on here not as a corporation here, or a corporation there, that does some-thing bad, or isn't so good. We're talking about a corporate system.

It's a system around which the whole of the United States is structured, and increasingly the world.

And it pops down in our communities. Because it's got to put its toxic dumps here, its factories here, and its banks here. It has to come into real life, and contact with the earth, and with people.

And once you enter a regulatory proceeding, under the Clean Air Act, or the Clean Water Act, or some kind of zoning issue, or land use issue, sprawl issue, or whatever it is, and you try to go into that proceeding and say: "We consider the granting of constitutional privileges and authority to corporations as unconstitutional and immoral and wrong." There's no room for that at that hearing. It's not on the table.[32]

I think it's amazing, how long people have gone in this country without provoking some real fundamental ferment of questioning how we resist, how we are being channelled.[33]

IV. The unchecked power of global corporations

Behind the scenes of the Millennium Meeting

In September 2000, Richard Grossman spoke at a teach-in on the growing global corporate influence over the United Nations, held in New York City by the International Forum on Globalization.

The United States is not a democracy. I don't think it's ever been a democracy.

And it's very painful to say that.

I think it's painful to hear it. I think we need to talk about it, and what the implications are. Because as we frame a problem, as we frame a question, so is shaped our response to it. So are shaped our goals, so are shaped our strategies and tactics. And so are determined the political arenas in which we want to struggle.

A few years ago, the people of Massachusetts passed a law. It wasn't the most radical law in history. It basically put some limits on the ability of state officials to use taxpayer money in Massachusetts to do business with companies doing business with the dictators in Burma. It wasn't a ban, it was a 'limitation.'

What happened?

Private power, in the institutional form of the corporation, nullified that law.

This law allegedly was about democracy in Burma. What the process demonstrated, was that there wasn't democracy in Massachusetts. Or the United States.

Here's what happened.

A shill non-profit corporation, a propaganda corporation

called the National Foreign Trade Council, which is made up of global corporations from all around the world, went right to federal court after the law was passed and said: "This law is beyond the authority of the people of Massachusetts to pass. We want you to declare it unconstitutional." A federal court immediately put an injunction on the law.

The state appealed and went to the Supreme Court. In June, by a vote of nine to nothing, meaning it was a triviality, the Supreme Court declared the law unconstitutional.

If that's not an example of private wealth nullifying, over-turning, kicking around, the people of Massachusetts, I don't know what is.

What's as important is the logic here, of the courts. Because basically what they're saying is: that a public, constitution-alized commonwealth, Massachusetts, may not establish criteria for how to spend its money. But a so-called 'private corporation' may.

A private corporation, a business corporation, *it* can have criteria, because it's private and governed by private law. But a public entity, a state government, constitutionalized, with elections, a legislature, judiciary, executive, all these things -- a Bill of Rights -- which we have in Massachusetts, that's contrary, that's beyond the authority of the people. ...

The Supreme Court of course cited the United States' Constitution as its authority in declaring this unconstitu-tional.

Because why? Because the court found them to be legal persons, a century ago.

Because they are centers of wealth and power, they are in fact trampling upon our fundamental rights. And in totality, it is our fundamental right to govern ourselves.

That's what's going on here. We can't say that when corporations pollute or when corporations do this, or all the long list of things that we'll be hearing today, that these are assaults on democracy, or corrosion of democracy, or subversions of democracy.

These are evidence of no democracy.

Otherwise they wouldn't be happening. Otherwise there would be remedies for this. Ones that don't involve ten years of organizing on single issue after single issue after single issue. This toxic here, and that dump there, and that new technology here, and genetically modified foods there.

So in one sense it's kind of terrifying, because we do not control our government. We never have. The Constitution was written for a minority of people, of propertied people, to control this country. And they made it incredibly difficult for when the 80 percent of human beings, of bipeds, who were defined as non-persons in the Constitution, eventually became legal persons, they made it extraordinarily difficult for the majority ever to really govern in this country.

And it's extraordinary to go back and look at even the debates around the ratification of the Constitution. Sometimes I've been accused: "You're using the values of today to judge dead people of 200 years ago."

Baloney! There were plenty of live people 200 years ago who judged the other live people. Based on their criteria, their values. And you go back and look at the debate over the ratification of the Constitution, which was, by the way, the first 'fast-track,' because they couldn't change it. All they could do was vote it up or down.

And you had a lot of people saying: "Hey, this is not what we had in mind! This is a plan for a global commercial empire." Some very prescient people back then (saying): "The

Supreme Court is going to be property's safety net unto eternity."

What kind of democratic process is it, when you give the final say to judges? In none of the 13 states during the period of the Articles of Confederation, was there a court that could overrule a legislature.

That was a totally new contrivance.

So what we have is a structural problem, where the rights of the majority to govern ourselves don't exist, have been diminished.

And the ability of a minority, working through their major political and economic vehicles, the corporation, is enormous. And their rights have been increased by the courts and legislatures over the last 200 years.

So we have a problem. We turn to our government for a remedy, as we're taught to do. But our government is complicit in the harms. Our government is complicit in the fundamental denial of our rights: as people, as citizens, as the sovereign people. As the source of all political power in this country is "We the People."

When the revolutionaries seized sovereignty from England, they didn't take the sovereignty of the king and put it in the state governments. They didn't put it in the federal governments. They said: "The sovereignty goes to the people."

Well, 80 percent of the people weren't people, but that's been taken care of. It's our job. It's our work!

So on the one hand, that should come as a terrifying idea. It also should come as something of a relief. Because if in fact we're not running this country, if in fact we don't have the authority to run this country, if we're not capable of acting like the sovereign people, of being 'we the people,' isn't it extraordinarily logical that through the course of the last century we're resisting one assault after another?

Endlessly, relentlessly: one technology, another technology, one war, another war, one buying of a candidate, one buying of campaigns. Aren't you tired of having to master all these technologies, and all this data and all this information? We're always on the defensive. We turn to our government for redress -- and they're on the other side.

So we have to figure out a different way. And one of the exciting things to me of the last couple years, especially since Seattle, this new ferment that's growing up. That is I think in this country, where the consciousness is not high, because we're the center of empire. We're the last to hear everything.

People in other countries know a lot more than we do about what our government is doing, about what our country's doing. (*Applause*)

******

Either you have democracy, where the people govern, or you don't have democracy, you have a plutocracy, or you have something else. ...

So we need to make some very powerful adjustments in our analysis and in our tactics and our strategies, in this country. Because we are not only resisting the global corporations, but we are also resisting the minority of propertied people in this country that control these corporations, and through the corporations, control the government. And control our minds and propaganda.

I make no distinction between giant corporations. There's no such thing as a good corporation or a better corporation. And it's nothing personal.

Corporations exist to concentrate power and wealth. They exist to rule: that's their function, that's their purpose. And nowadays they rule with the cover of law, with the protection of the law. And I guess they always have in this country.

When our learned judges need to find something in the Constitution -- even though the word corporation doesn't appear in the Constitution – when they need to find that corporations have intangible property rights, or that the corporation is a person, or that a corporate charter is a contract protected by the Constitution, or need to find that the Commerce Clause protects the corporation from state intervention -- they'll find it.

So, in closing, I would say that we need to nurture in this country a democracy movement. You know, sometimes, very often, people come from other countries and say: "We're building a democracy movement in our country, will you help us?"

And we do. And our heart goes out to them. And we're not offended that they don't have democracy in their country. Well, how do we build a democracy movement in our country? Maybe we can learn from folks in other countries.

But we have to nurture this. We have to go from this single issue struggle, single issue after single issue, technology after technology, one corporation after another corporation, the buying of this politician, the buying of that politician.

To saying: how do we take control of our government? Not 'take back,' because we've never had it. So we have to do something that's new.

How do we start our own city councils, and our own state and county legislatures? How do we *challenge* the notion that the corporation is a person? And *challenge* the Commerce Clause and *challenge* the Contract Clause and *challenge* all the rationalizations they put forward to say we have no authority?

A couple of years ago I had the good fortune to meet with Thomas Berry. Some of you may know his book about the origin of the planet; he's a cosmologist.

And he said: "What are you boys up to?" He's about 85, he can call us that. And I said "well," -- this was from my perspective four or five years ago -- "we want to eliminate the thousand largest corporations from the face of the earth."

He looked at us for a very long time. He was thinking, geologic time, he was thinking. And he said to us: "Why do you have such low aspirations?"[34]

(laughter and applause)

V. Where do we go from here?

Reconceptualizing Our Work

How can we reconceptualize our work; teach ourselves to see how we got into these messes; rethink goals and campaigns and arenas of struggle and language and assumptions, and the daily work of educating, organizing?

If in fact we start working more democratically, then people could say: "Well, what is it we want, and what is it we need, and how do we want to produce them?"

Right now how we produce products is off the public agenda. They are private decisions. We have no authority. And you can see that more historically, in the global so-called trade agreements. Because in the global trade agreements the language is very explicit. Whereas here it is sort of case law and corporate doctrine.

The global treaties cannot address the question of how a product is produced and how labor is organized. It may not address that subject. That's why the phoniness of putting these labor and environmental side agreements is just like bullshit regulation, regulating how many people are going to be killed and how many people exploited.

But that's the core of American law since the 1880s or so. That it's private law, it's off the agenda. Our elected officials have no authority to address those questions.

So we have to seize that authority, and say: "Well, we'll decide, in some democratic fashion, what's going to be made and how it's made."[35]

We've been resisting corporate assaults one at a time, after the fact, and over and over and over again. It's enough! It's time to build a cosmic democracy movement. A movement for political rights and for real self-government. It's time for *us* to be 'socially responsible.' It's time for *us* to be 'accountable.'[36]

The corporate state, like the slave state, is a creation of the law. It is backed by the law, it is backed by the army, it is backed by that kind of language from the Supreme Court. Every time we go up against that, we go up against our own government. That's what the corporate state is.

Every time we concede that corporations have the right to a permit to pollute to an acceptable level, we give it all away, we validate the system. Every time we concede that when you go to work you have to give up your constitutional rights, we validate the system, we feed into it.

So if we want to make some incremental gains, yes, we can do some good, by cutting down some pollution. But we have to do it in a different way, that doesn't lock us into a dead end. That begins to open up the whole thing.

You see, when people keep turning to this Congress, and to the federal system to regulate, and keep supporting this whole constitutional structure of law we have, it makes it much more difficult for the people at the local level, where the corporate state comes down like a tornado, to dump and diss, and deny rights. It validates all of that, it creates more barriers.[37]

Maybe we can legitimate, in this bastion of corporate and capital control, the idea that a free people don't have to internalize the corporate culture.

That we can believe that what exists now was not inevitable, is not irreversible, is the most efficient, leads to the most freedom, and all that junk.

That we don't have to concede that the laws of the market supercede the laws that free human beings, sentient human beings coming together to negotiate with each other can make.

We have to remember that we, that free people, do not negotiate with governments, we don't negotiate with corporations. We negotiate with one another.

And I think we need to shift from these cultures of resistance to harms, one at a time, or to save one forest at a time, or to fight one corporation at a time -- to cultures of struggle which are about self-governance.

That the vision is self-governance, and the path will come out of the struggles people are involved with, all the time.

Frederick Douglass said: "Power concedes nothing without a struggle. Not to believe that, is to believe that we can harvest crops without plowing the ground."

Now what makes me optimistic is, I don't think for a hundred years that we have thought about, in a serious long-term way, engaging in struggle for self-government against the concentrated powers that are arrayed against us.

And that is something we are beginning to do, and the corporations are the path into that.[38]

But it's not about the corporation. It's about us: who we are, what we want, what our responsibilities are as human beings on this earth and in this country. What our responsibilities are to the people who came before us and to the other creatures of the world, that cannot speak and act for themselves.

And it's about being ready to take some very different steps, related to violating what's called 'settled law.' There's been no movement worth its salt, starting with the Levellers, going through the American Revolution, the abolition movement, the workers' movement, civil rights movement, gay and lesbian movement, where the people in these movements have agreed with the fundamental basis of the laws that were oppressing them.[39]

"It will not happen in the State of New York": criminalize fracking

Richard Grossman's talk at the Frackbusters New York workshop in the Community Church of New York on October 1, 2011 was his last public presentation.

The three topics I'm going to talk about will be:

One: How peoples' history tells us that we've got to rip this struggle out of the regulatory and administrative structure of law, out of the Department of Environmental Conservation. And why that is necessary and true.

Secondly: Why we're choosing to write our own law, and push that law, and present that law to our officials and to people across the state. And why that law is a criminalizing law. Why that law criminalizes fracking, the corporate frackers, and all related fracking activities.

And thirdly, I'm going to lay out my, and the Frackbusters' sense -- it's in an early stage yet – but how we see the next six months to a year playing out. How we're going to drive this across the state.

For my whole generation -- and I see other grey haired people here: our generation has been channeled into these agencies, on issue after issue. Think of it: the Nuclear Regulatory Commission; the toxic substance laws, the federal and state laws on toxics; the energy commissions. They all set up the same kind of a process, channeling us into an arena where the deck is stacked.

So that's the bigger picture. The state and the United States are not neutral in any of these realms, but particularly when it comes to regulatory administrative law: the deck is stacked...

Let me compare what happens in a regulatory administrative arena, and what happens in, say – just out of the blue – a 'criminal' arena. First of all, in the regulatory arena, passion and emotion are not allowed. Because it's all about so-called 'science' and 'the facts.'

And we can't question the history of the corporation...The only issue on the table is: Are the harms that people can predict powerful enough that they need to be mitigated a little bit? And how much is it going to cost to mitigate them, and is that feasible or practicable? That's all that it's about. When we go into the regulatory administrative arenas we have no authority. We just talk about the geology and the hydrology, that's it. We say to the hearing officer, "we want to challenge and contest the notion that the business corporation is wrapped in the Fourteenth Amendment." He says: "I have nothing to do with that. That's outside the purview of these hearings. It's not relevant."

We want to talk about broader energy policy in New York State. "That's not relevant. You can't talk about that here. You want to talk hydrology and geology? We'll talk about that."

So in SPAN, our group in Ulster and Greene Counties, and then in Frackbusters New York, we decided that we are going to rip this whole process out of that realm. That's not about us, that's not about sovereignty. And we're going to take it, force it, drive it into the arenas of sovereignty across the state.

Our groups are made up of people from many groups around the state who have risen up to challenge the idea of fracking, towards prohibiting it, not making it less bad, but prohibiting and preventing. And so we have decided to move the struggle into the legislature and into all arenas, including local legislatures, including the body politic, including the media. And unite around the concept that corporate fracking is criminal behavior.[40]

Abolish the corporation
An Act To Criminalize Chartered, Incorporated Business Entities

Richard L. Grossman October 2011
a work-in-progress

As of 12:01 a.m. on July 4, 2012, no incorporated business shall exist or operate within the United States and its territories, or within any State or municipality.

As of 12:01 a.m. on July 4, 2012, all existing business corporation charters granted by the United States, and by all States, shall be null and void.

Neither the United States nor any State shall issue new charters for incorporated businesses. Any chartered, incorporated business entity -- domestic, foreign, alien -- existing and operating after the above date shall be deemed a violent, criminal, and terrorist conspiracy. Its directors and executive officers must be charged with ecocide, criminal conspiracy and crimes against humanity.

No directors or executive officers of unchartered, unincorporated business entities which may succeed outlawed chartered, incorporated business entities shall be empowered, enabled or protected..[41]

From the last interview

The Corporate Crime Reporter *published the last interview with Richard Grossman on October 17, 2011. (Excerpted here)*

For me, our challenge is teaching ourselves to see beyond each single corporate state invasion and assault and denial to recognize the structures of usurpation that have long been in place – structures of usurpation, of illegitimate governance, that activists with only rare exceptions over the past four-score years have confronted.

The second part of that challenge is this – people who have been taught to mobilize against single corporate state assaults – one at a time and over and over again – start revealing and dismantling those structures, the constitutional and mythological underpinnings of "we the people's" disempowerment.

And begin replacing them with values and governance structures designed to maximize liberty for the earth and biological systems and other species, while engendering healthy humility for the human species. ...

The essence of the power arrayed against the 99 percent are structures of minority-rule governance deeply rooted, honored and celebrated, even by, I suspect, many of the people who are occupying Wall Street today.

I'm referring to the great myths of this nation's founding and founders, of the U.S. Constitution and constitutional jurisprudence, the nonsense about limited governance, the sanctification of "the rule of law" when lawmaking and interpreting and enforcing have been the special preserve in every generation of a small minority.

I'm talking about the private ordering of economic decision-making, the sweeping constitutional privileges wielded by directors of the "creatures of law" we call chartered, incorporated businesses camouflaged as "free enterprise" and "the invisible hand."

I see the Constitution as a minority rule document....
The people of my generation – I'm almost 70 – we've been struggling against corporate and government assaults one after another, corporate and government wars – one after another, against usurpations galore engineered by corporate directors.

Where can we turn for remedy? What political, constitutional mechanisms can we use to undo accumulated usurpations of the past, to start governing ourselves, our communities, our states, our nation?

For people who see these constant assaults and denials – defined by our corporate, Earth-gobbling culture as "legal" and "necessary" for freedom, jobs and progress – for people agitating to stop these wars, to stop the destruction of our communities and escalating inequalities, to launch sane and just transitions in energy, food – don't we have to reconceptualize our work as humans on this Earth?

One of the tasks for my generation before we leave the scene is to engage younger generations about all this, starting off with this central terrifying point – we've lost.

Fifty years ago, forty years ago, those of us who started off being very active against all kinds of injustices, we had a very different picture of what this country could be like in 2011.

Today, we're not even close.

Not for lack of struggle, persistence, tenacity.

So what happened? What's to be learned from the past half-century of organizing and resistance and electioneering and law-writing? [42]

VI. "Don't try it at home alone."

Interviewer (2010): You mention dismantling the accumulations of the past. That's difficult... Is it about recognizing first of all what happened?

RG: Well, that's essential! So that means to begin having the discussion. It's kind of boring, to say: "Oh, all these horrible things are happening, and maybe some of the ideals and aspirations we had haven't come to fruition." Well that's kind of terrifying and depressing.

And then people say: "Well, what to do?" And I say, "We have to have some very different conversations, about the past, our own work and the nature of the problems that we face." And that's really boring, and diversionary, and all that.

But I think: How do people come together to rethink the work and conceptualize a different direction, and different goals, without talking, fighting, arguing for a while?

Let's look at the Constitution again... Has it been an impediment? Or has it been our savior, as many people on the left even would say. I think those are very challenging questions to grapple with. [43]

When a new movement arises... there needs to be a flowering of new activist organizing, friendly and conducive to the kind of creativity that is now essential.

The human, daily work of creating something new is very different from critiquing the old or trying to make the old a little less bad. [44]

One thing that's becoming clearer and clearer to me, is that the goal is really people. And I think it's very similar to how the abolitionists viewed their work.

The goal is engaging more and more people in these conversations. The goal is helping each other to un-colonize our minds. Our goal is to help each other to think, so that we can see what it is we are immersed in.

So that when we come together, committed to actually do some organizing, to do some work, to pour our energy and our courage and our commitment into some communal effort... if we win, it actually wins something. And if we lose, we also win, because it reveals what's going on.[45]

So we've got a lot to undo: really a couple of millennia to undo. Of the few ruling the many. It didn't just start in the United States. There's a lot of work to be done. And a lot of the work is up here (*points to head*).

And I would say: "Don't try it at home alone. You need other people to do that work."

And we're going to have to be violating what they say is the law, and what they say is the lore.

And we're going to have to put ourselves in a place where they say: "You're a traitor. Because you're preventing freedom, and you're preventing security, you're preventing jobs, you're preventing growth, you're preventing all the great things that we know is the heart of America."[46]

Here's what I want to leave you with: that the fundamental decision-making that defines our lives, and defines our community, that defines life and death, war and peace, has been defined as beyond our authority, as private. And is shielded by the Constitution, shielded by the courts. Our own Constitution being used against us.

So in all the organizing and educating we do, we need to understand how that works and challenge it -- as we try to stop the particular assault. If we don't do that, then we're opening ourselves up to being in the same boat, time after time after time. It's we who have to change, not the corporations. We have to change how we think, what we know, and what we do.[47]

Our venue is the Village Square. Our venue is the streets, our venue is our legislatures. We make the law. That is our responsibility, as the sovereign people...The people are the source of all political power in this country. But it's not true until we exercise our power. It's not true until we exercise our rights. It is only we who can do that.

It's not about the corporate leaders. It's not about the corporations. It's about us and what kind of government we impose, because we organize enough, and are smart, persistent and stubborn enough, and intelligent enough to actually demand and then get what we want.

And not leave it to somebody else to define us, and say: "This is all you can ask for."

Thank you very much.[48]

VII.
Richard Grossman and his work:
on-line remembrances

November - December 2011

August 1996

Dave Henson, a founding member of *Program on Corpo-rations, Law and Democracy* (POCLAD). (*Henson, More-house and Coleridge excerpts are from* "Reflections on Richard Grossman: A tribute to Richard's life from the POCLAD colleagues," *https://www.poclad.org/BWA/2011/BWA_2011_DEC.html*)

Richard was a direct and profound inspiration for thousands of activists and people of conscience. Through his writings and the organizations he founded and co-founded, includ-ing in the mid-1980's the Highlander Center's STP Program ("Stop the Pollution, Save the Planet"), in 1994 the Program on Corporations, Law and Democracy (POCLAD), and in 2007 the "Democracy Schools" [co-created with CELDF.org], Richard has helped lead tens of thousands more people to a clearer historical, cultural and legal analysis of the structural causes of – and potential remedies to – persistent social and economic disparity in power and wealth between We The People and the political and economic institutions the People are meant to govern.

.... This past couple of months I have been thinking a lot of Richard. I hear the direct and indirect influence of Richard Grossman every day in the "Occupy Movement". I'm sure he had quite a critique of everything "occupy", but I know he must have relished in the increasingly widespread conscious dissent he has helped instigate. Long Live the Love, Passion and Ideas of Richard Grossman!

Ward Morehouse, co-founder, POCLAD (1929 - 2012)

I first met Richard in a group called Communities Concerned about Corporations...
The group ran from March 1991 to Dec. 1995 when ...
Richard and I went on to begin organizing POCLAD. Peter Montague (author, activist, publisher of Rachel's Weekly) was an active collaborator. It was a large and loose-knit group -- a five year attempt to form a coalition of

communities, workers, injured workers and investors affected by the oil and chemical industries to engage in two party bargaining with the individual corporations in the industry.

Richard came to Communities Concerned from a long background of activism, most recently some 20 years in the anti-nuclear movement where he learned hard lessons about head banging against specific corporations. We made common cause as I was learning those same lessons from my then ten-year struggle against the corporate criminals responsible for the Bhopal tragedy.

One of our projects together was a Nov. 1994 letter that Richard, Peter Montague and I wrote to the leaders of the 15 largest environmental organizations, also signed by some 400 environmental activists, asking these leaders to meet with us to talk about the threat of corporations to the entire environmental movement. (See "A Letter to Friends," at: *https://ratical.org/corporations/REHW407.html)*

Russell Mokhiber, *Corporate Crime Reporter*

...When I interviewed him last month, Grossman was in Sweden visiting his daughter. I asked him how he was doing.

He said that he had been diagnosed earlier in the year with melanoma. He asked me not to mention it to anyone. He said he was being treated and he would be fine.

It was not to be.[49]

Greg Coleridge, POCLAD, Ohio

Richard Grossman passed away on Tuesday, November 22. The movement we know today to end never-intended constitutional rights for corporations as a step toward real self-governance was birthed, grew and developed to a great extent by this remarkable, complex human being with a deep passion and love for nature, humanity and justice. He influenced and inspired thousands directly, an incalculable number more indirectly. Richard and Ward Morehouse started the Program on Corporations, Law & Democracy

(POCLAD) in 1994, a combined think tank and breeding ground for activist experimentation to challenge corporate rule. His work in this field originated with the publication of *Taking Care of Business: Citizenship and the Charter of Incorporation*, which he co-authored with Frank Adams in 1993.

Richard reveled in reading, thinking, writing and discussing on what had been for more than a century of buried history and analysis on how corporations (creations of the state) came to acquire power and rights that were presented by the culture as inevitable and irreversible. POCLAD semi-annual retreats among the dozen collective "principles" were serious extended weekends in "grappling" and "rethinking" the relationship between people and our own legal creations — conveying that the ultimate inhibitor to self-governance weren't corporations but us — what we've come to accept and what we're willing to do. He dug deep in history, law and scholars that most people in the present had never heard of and/or who seemed quaint or arcane.

Richard was rigorous and demanded the same from everyone who took ending corporate rights seriously. He challenged as well as supported. He demanded as well as suggested. He knocked our ideas and conceptions down as well as worked collaboratively to build up others. He was uncompromising on core concepts but engaged in genuine give and take that helped him evolve from primarily advocating revoking individual corporate charters, to ending corporate constitutional rights (personhood) at the national level, to asserting democratic "right to decide" control over corporations through municipal ordinances, to criminalizing chartered incorporated business entities. You didn't always agree with Richard but you were always mentally stretched and challenged to defend your unconsciously accepted doctrines.

Marty Teitel, *Saltmarshmarty.blogspot.de*

...my role model in cranky-tude was certainly Richard Lee Grossman. And I say this with the greatest of affection. I suspect Richard's basic belief was that there is nothing unserious about injustice and suffering. I was never in his presence without being exposed to his outrage, which always included me as an object as well as a subject...

I think Richard believed there was something pro-social about being irate at actions and above all corporations he considered to be misbehaving or wrong.

From the NY Times guestbook: November 30, 2011

"I never met Richard, but am a great admirer of his work. Please accept my condolences."
Juliet Schor

"Richard lay the foundation for so much of the work happening today in the spheres of corporate accountability, income equality and environmental and social justice. Thank you Richard."
Annie Leonard, The Story of Stuff Project Berkeley, California. November 29, 2011

"I learned so much from Richard over the years. His clear vision was an inspiration to me and others. I still remember his pushing those of us on the National Council of Churches' Eco-justice working group to challenge corporate polluters more. He will be missed but his legacy lives."
Jaydee Hanson, Arlington, Virginia

****

David Bollier, *www.bollier.org*

Richard Grossman was one of those activist eccentrics who took democratic power so seriously that he knowingly marginalized himself. Mainstream political culture regarded his positions as crazy or tactically unwise -- but eventually the world began to catch up with him... The leitmotif of Grossman's work is well-stated by a standing feature on the POCLAD website called, "By Whose Authority?"

Grossman ultimately decided that revoking corporate personhood was not enough; the corporate form itself needed to be outlawed. So he wrote a four-page draft bill. "If people want to go into business, fine," Grossman told the Corporate Crime Reporter. "But this law would strip away 500 years of Constitutional protections and privileges. No more limited liability for shareholders. No more perpetual life. No more Constitutional protections." Now that's a free market!

If Grossman was often accused of being inflexible, his unwavering views showed how impotent the "flexible" approaches to corporate reform had been over the course of decades. Corporations simply annexed more and more legal authority at the expense of democracy and ordinary citizens. POCLAD's legal and historical analysis helped shine a bright light on this fact, and educate people about democratic powers that had been lost.

Richard Grossman passed away on November 22, 2011, at age 68. His legacy will surely live on as the Occupy movement and others probe more deeply into the sources of democratic disempowerment and wealth inequality.[50]

David C. Maas, Bellingham, WA

Sometimes we fail to recognize the importance of a person's work until after his or her life has ended. Richard Grossman, who died in November, is a good example.

"Fish Discover Water Last": SOURCE MATERIALS

The text of this booklet is mainly 'woven' with excerpts from the editor's transcriptions of Richard Grossman's recorded speeches, workshops and interviews, listed below. Links have been updated as possible for the 2021 publication, or removed if no longer available.

RICHARD GROSSMAN SPEAKS: 1995-2011

1995
"Dismantling Corporations" Part one of a TUC Radio tribute to Richard Grossman's work by Maria Gilardin. Recorded at a July 1995 International Forum on Globalization retreat meeting. 29 minutes. *http://www.radio4all.net/index.php/program/56288*

1996
"Dismantling Corporations." Part two of a TUC Radio tribute to Richard Grossman's work by Maria Gilardin. Recorded at the July 1996 International Forum on Globalization teach-in, Washington, D.C. 29 minutes. http://*www.radio4all.net/index.php/program/56477*

"Democracy and the Historical Relationship Between Citizens and Corporations"
Presentation at International Forum on Globalization Global teach-in 2: The social, ecological, cultural and political costs of economic globalization. May 10-12, 1996, Washington, D.C.

1997
"Defining the Corporation, Defining Ourselves"
Recorded at the University of Colorado in Boulder on February 13, 1997. 1hr:41min
https://www.youtube.com/watch?v=cTLbR37T3_A

2000
"Behind the scenes of the Millennium Meeting:
Unchecked power of global corporations." New York,
September 2000, presentation at an International Forum on
Globalization teach-in on growing global corporate influence
over the United Nations. Recorded by Maria Gilardin of TUC
Radio.

2001
"Defying Corporations" Talk by the late Jane Anne
Morris and Richard Grossman of the Program on
Corporations, Law and Democracy (POCLAD), recorded
October 8, 2001 at Gowen Hall on the University of
Washington campus in Seattle.18:45 min.
https://www.youtube.com/watch?v=_yjWbojwbOg

2003
"Model Amici Curiae Brief to Eliminate Corporate Rights" by
Richard L. Grossman, Thomas Linzey, Esq., and Daniel E.
Brannen, Jr., Esq.
www.ratical.org/corporations/demoBrief.html

2005
Challenging Corporate Law and Lore, talk given
February 10, 2005 in Seattle, Washington. 57:42 min.
https://www.youtube.com/watch?v=OTpGzdc3ZFI

Followed by Q&A from the talks by Thomas Linzey with the
Community Environmental Legal Defense Fund and Richard
Grossman. 23:04 min.

2006
**"When Injustice is Legal, what do the Abolitionists
teach us about challenging corporate rule?"** Antioch
College, Yellow Springs, Ohio, Nov. 2006, parts 1 and 2, TUC
radio download, 29 min.
*https://tucradio.org/?s=richard+grossman&submit=Sear
ch*

2007

"Constitutionalizing Freedom" talk at the TAMING THE GIANT CORPORATION: A National Conference on Corporate Accountability, Friday, June 8, 2007, Washington, D.C. Followed by "Strategies to Subordinate Corporations: A Discussion About What Works," Friday evening conference workshop. June 8, 2007. (Videos no longer online)

2009

Richard Grossman on Earth Jurisprudence
Gaia Foundation, U.K., Sept. 2009. Richard Grossman gives his views on Earth Jurisprudence, the concept first introduced by Thomas Berry. 3:03 min.
Youtube: *http://tinyurl.com/b5jbmg7*

2010

Interview at Left Forum 2010, Pace University, New York City, March 20, 2010. Follows presentation at workshop: "Strategizing to Build Real Self-Governance." (link removed)

2011

Richard L. Grossman: Presentation at the Frackbusters New York's first Criminalizing Fracking workshop, Oct. 1, 2011, Community Church of New York. 28:23 min.
https://www.youtube.com/watch?v=h6UK_7rmy7I

"An Act To Criminalize Chartered, Incorporated Business Entities." October 2011. Full text at:
https://ratical.org/corporations/AtCCIBE.html

Interview with Richard Grossman, West Hurley, New York. Corporate Crime Reporter, published on October 17, 2011.
https://ratical.org/corporations/CCRivRG1011.html

ENDNOTES

See Source Materials for more information, links where active

1) Richard Grossman: "When Injustice is legal, what do the Abolitionists teach us about challenging corporate rule?" Antioch College, November, 2006, part 1.

2) Richard Grossman: "Constitutionalizing Freedom." Talk at TAMING THE GIANT CORPORATION: A National Conference on Corporate Accountability, Washington, D.C. June 8, 2007.

3) Richard Grossman: "When Injustice is Legal." Antioch College, November, 2006, part 1.

4) Richard Grossman: "When Injustice is Legal, what do the Abolitionists teach us about challenging corporate rule?" Antioch College, November, 2006, part 2.

5) "Democracy and the Historical Relationship Between Citizens and Corporations," Washington, D.C. International Forum on Globalization, May, 1996.

6) Ibid.

7) Richard Grossman: "Challenging Corporate Law and Lore," Speech in Seattle, Washington, February 10, 2005.

8) "Democracy and the Historical Relationship Between Citizens and Corporations." May, 1996.

9) Richard Grossman: "When Injustice is Legal." Antioch College, November, 2006, part 2.

10) Richard Grossman: "When Injustice is Legal." Antioch College, November, 2006, part 1.

11) Richard Grossman: "When Injustice is Legal." Antioch College, November, 2006, part 2.

12) Richard Grossman - "Challenging Corporate Law and Lore," Speech in Seattle, Washington, February 10, 2005.

13) Richard Grossman: "When Injustice is Legal." Antioch College, November 2006, part 1.

14) Richard Grossman: "Challenging Corporate Law and Lore." Speech in Seattle, Washington, February 10, 2005.

15) From "Model Amici Curiae Brief to Eliminate Corporate Rights" by Richard L. Grossman, Thomas Linzey, Esq., and Daniel E. Brannen, Jr., Esq. 2003:
"After political expedience convinced Abraham Lincoln to use the Civil War to outlaw slavery, people forced the federal government to pass the Civil Rights Act of 1866 and constitutional amendments to give rights to newly freed slaves, which the drafters of the Constitution failed to define as "persons." [29] Adopted in 1868, Section 1 of the Fourteenth Amendment says:

All persons born or naturalized in the United States, and subject to the jurisdiction thereof, are citizens of the United States and of the State wherein they reside. No State shall make or enforce any law which shall abridge the privileges or immunities of citizens of the United States; nor shall any state deprive any person of life, liberty, or property, without due process of law; nor deny to any person within its jurisdiction the equal protection of the laws.

The guarantees of the Fourteenth Amendment have been expanded to include a litany of personal liberty rights. [30] Working for corporate clients enriched and empowered by the Civil War, lawyers began persuading judges to use the language of the Fourteenth Amendment to overturn state legislation originally intended to subordinate corporations. Their efforts led to a transformation of the law, undermining the republican frame of governance. As Justice Brennan has declared, "by 1871, it was well understood that corporations should be treated as natural persons for virtually all purposes of constitutional and statutory analysis." Monell v. Department of Social Services of the City of New York, 436 U.S. 658, 687 (1978).

Continue to read a more detailed description of how corporations ended up considered as 'persons' by the Supreme Court in 1886 and 1889, at: https://ratical.org/corporations/demoBrief.html

16) Richard Grossman: „Constitutionalizing Freedom." Talk at TAMING THE GIANT CORPORATION, Washington, D.C. June 8, 2007.

17) See III.A. "Finding" Corporations in the Fourteenth Amendment," in a draft legal brief by Richard L. Grossman, Thomas Linzey, Esq., and Daniel E. Brannen, Jr., Esq. © 2003.

18) Richard Grossman: "Challenging Corporate Law and Lore." Speech in Seattle, Washington, February 10, 2005.

19) Richard Grossman: "Dismantling Corporations." Presentation at International Forum on Globalization retreat meeting, 1995. For more on the Populists see: "The Populist Moment: A Short History of the Agrarian Revolt in America," by Lawrence Goodwyn, November, 1978.

20) Richard Grossman: "Challenging Corporate Law and Lore." Seattle, Washington, February 10, 2005.

21) "Democracy and the Historical Relationship Between Citizens and Corporations." May, 1996, Washington, D.C.

22) Richard Grossman: "Challenging Corporate Law and Lore." Seattle, Washington, February 10, 2005. Question & answer session.

23) Richard Grossman: "Challenging Corporate Law and Lore," Speech in Seattle, Washington, February 10, 2005.

24) Ibid.

25) Richard Grossman's presentation at the Frackbusters New York's first "Criminalizing Fracking" workshop, New York, October 1, 2011.

26) Richard Grossman: "Challenging Corporate Law and Lore." Seattle, Washington, February 10, 2005.

27) "Criminalizing Fracking" workshop, October 1, 2011.

28) Richard Grossman: "Challenging Corporate Law and Lore." Seattle, Washington, February 10, 2005.

29) For background see: "History of the Federal Judiciary: The Debs Case: Labor, Capital, and the Federal Courts of the 1890s:"
www.fjc.gov/history/home.nsf/page/tu_debs_narrative. html

30) Workshop presentation and discussion on "Strategies to Subordinate Corporations: A Discussion About What Works" at the TAMING THE GIANT CORPORATION conference, Washington, D.C. June 8, 2007.

31) Richard Grossman: "Dismantling Corporations." International Forum on Globalization retreat meeting. July, 1995.

32) Richard Grossman: "When Injustice is Legal, what do the Abolitionists teach us about challenging corporate rule?"part 2, Antioch College, November, 2006. TUC Radio

33) Richard Grossman: "Challenging Corporate Law and Lore." Seattle, Washington, February 10, 2005.

34) "Behind the scenes of the Millennium Meeting," International Forum on Globalization teach-in, New York City, September 2000.

35) "Challenging Corporate Law and Lore." Q & A, Seattle, February 10, 2005.

36) "Democracy and the Historical Relationship Between Citizens and Corporations." Washington, D.C., May 10-12, 1996.

37) Friday evening workshop at TAMING THE GIANT CORPORATION Conference. June 8, 2007.

38) Richard Grossman: "Dismantling Corporations," International Forum on Globalization retreat meeting, July 1995.

39) Richard Grossman: "Challenging Corporate Law and Lore." Seattle, Washington, February 10, 2005.

40) "Criminalizing Fracking" workshop, October 1, 2011.

41) "An Act To Criminalize Chartered, Incorporated Business Entities." October 2011.

42) Interview with Richard Grossman. *Corporate Crime Reporter*, October 2011.

43) Interview at New Left Forum 2010, March 20, 2010.

44) Richard Grossman on Earth Jurisprudence. Gaia Foundation meeting, U.K., September 2009.
45) "When Injustice is Legal." Part 2, November 2006.

46) "Challenging Corporate Law and Lore." Seattle, Washington, February 10, 2005.

47) "Defying Corporations." Talk by Jane Anne Morris and Richard Grossman, October 8, 2001. Seattle.

48) "Challenging Corporate Law and Lore." Seattle, Washington, February 10, 2005.

49) *Corporate Crime Reporter,* November 25, 2011. "Richard Grossman 1943-2011" *https://corporatecrimereporter.com/richardgrossman11252011.htm*

50) David Bollier, "Richard Grossman, Remembered," December 23, 2011. *http://www.bollier.org/richard-grossman-remembered*

APPENDIX

Books, publications

Richard Kazis, Richard L. Grossman, *Fear at Work: Job Blackmail, Labor, and the Environment* (Pilgrim Press, 1982).

Richard Lee Grossman, Frank T. Adams, *TAKING CARE OF BUSINESS: Citizenship and the Charter of Incorporation* (Charter Ink, 1993). Out of print but online at: *http://www.ratical.org/corporations/TCoB.html*

Dean Ritz, editor. *Defying Corporations, Defining Democracy: A Book of History & Strategies* (Apex Press, 2001). Includes key chapters by Richard Grossman.

Articles, essays, letters, from the *ratical.org* archive

Many of Richard Grossman's writings from 1988 to 2011 are listed and available online at *https://ratical.org/corporations/RLG1943-2011.html*, following David Ratcliffe's "In Memoriam: Richard Grossman 1943-2011."

- The Saturation of the South, *The Egg*, Summer 1988

- The Song and Dance of the 1990 Clean Air `Act', *New Solutions*, Winter 1991

- DEFIANCE! An Open Letter, April 1991, *The Wrenching Debate Gazette*

- *Taking Care Of Business - Citizenship and the Charter of Incorporation*, 1993

- Review of *TAKING CARE OF BUSINESS: Citizenship and the Charter of Incorporation*, Earth Island Journal, Spring 1993

- Taking Care of Business: The Corporate Crunch in Vermont, *Multinational Monitor*, July/August 1993

- Justice For Sale: Shortchanging the Public Interest for Private Gain, Book review by Richard Grossman, *The Workbook*, Fall 1993

- Ending Corporate Governance, reprinted from *San Diego Review*, October 1, 1994

- The Struggle for Democratic Control of Corporations: Taking the Offensive, from the Program on Corporations, Law, & Democracy

- Asserting Democratic Control Over Corporations: A Call to Lawyers, Richard L. Grossman and Ward More house, *The NATIONAL LAWYERS Guild Practitioner*, Fall 1995

- Playing By Whose Rules? A Challenge to Environmental, Civil Rights and Other Activists, *DAYBREAK*, 1995

- Letter to the Progressive's Editor, March 24, 1995

- Minorities, the Poor & Ending Corporate Rule, Richard L. Grossman and Ward Morehouse, Poverty & Race, September/October 1995

- January '96 letter re: 1996 Public Interest Environmental Law Conference, Richard L. Grossman and Ward Morehouse

- Corporations, Lawyers, Democracy, Justice & The Law, 9 Seminars, 1996 Public Interest Environmental Law Conference, University of Oregon Law School, March 7-10, 1996

- Transcript: "Revoking The Corporation", a discussion w/R. Grossman & W. Morehouse, Palo Alto, California, January 29, 1996

- Letter to Ralph Nader from Program on Corporations, Law & Democracy, February 29, 1996

- International Dairy Foods Association ET AL V. Attorney General of Vermont, on rBST labelling, August 15, 1996

- A Quick Look at What Happened in New Mexico, 1997. From Defying Corporations, Defining Democracy (2001), pp. 124-129

- Corporate Crime Reporter interview with POCLAD's Richard Grossman, November 18, 1997

- Letter to Akhil Reed Amar on Amar's book, *The Bill of Rights: Creation and Reconstruction*, December 30, 1998, from *Defying Corporations, Defining Democracy (2001), pp. 217-219*

- Uprooting "Growth" as Metaphor: 20th Century Reflections for the 21st, December 1999. An essay in 18 parts, all related to growth.

- Anti-Federalists Speak: Property vs. Democracy in 1787, Fall 1999

- The WTO, The US Constitution, and Self-Government. Originally published in POCLAD's *By What Authority* in Fall 1999, it was reprinted and extended in *Defying Corporations, Defining Democracy: A Book of History & Strategies* (2001). Mike Ferner, Dave Henson, Peter Kellman, Ward Morehouse and Mary Zepernick contributed to this article. "Written just before the historic WTO protests in Seattle, it has enduring insights concerning the role of corporations in trade agreements, finance and all manner of usurped governance."

• Rumors of USA Democracy Discovered to be Counterfeit. By Greg Coleridge, Richard Grossman, Mary Zepernick. Originally published in *By What Authority*, Fall 2000, Reprinted/extended in *Defying Corporations, Defining Democracy* (2001)

• Revolutionizing Corporate Law, from D*efying Corporations, Defining Democracy* (2001)

• The Strategy for Electricity is Democracy, January 30, 2001

• How Long Shall We Grovel?, A Memo for the Record, April 4, 2001

• Letter on the USA Patriot Act, We The People, Corporations and the U.S. Constitution, December 11, 2001

• When Corporations Wield the Constitution, November 2002. By Richard L. Grossman and Ward Morehouse. This appeared as the Foreward in George Drafan's *The Elite Consensus: When Corporations Wield the Constitution* (Apex Press: 2003)

• Letter to Joan Mulhern - *Earthjustice*, April 22, 2002, Earth Day

• Letter to Ralph Nader, September 10, 2002

- Letter to Sarah Ruth van Gelder, Editor, *Yes! A Journal of Positive Futures,* November 25, 2002

- Letter to *The Nation* on "Liberalizing The Law" by Alexander Wohl, June 11, 2003

- Who Were the Populists? - Richard Grossman on Bill Moyers' Speech, June 24, 2003

- Model Amici Curiae Brief to Eliminate Corporate Rights, by Richard L. Grossman, Thomas Linzey, Esq., and Daniel E. Brannen, Jr., Esq., 2003

- Letter on "Antigloblism's Jewish Problem" by Mark Strauss, December 23, 2003

- Letter to Morris Dickstein on Upton Sinclair and Beef Corporations, January 2, 2004

- American Tragedy: The Codification and Institutionalization of Violence, January 8, 2004

- Shifting into a Different Gear: Empowering Communities, Protecting the Environment, and Building Democracy by Asserting Local Control Over Factory Farm and Sludge Corporations in Pennsylvania, with Thomas Linzey, Esq., February 15, 2004

- Confronting the Corporate Constitution in Pennsylvania, June 2004

- Richard Grossman, Letter To An Environmental Filmmaker, August 6, 2004

- Richard Grossman, Letter To Nancy Jack Todd, September 18, 2004

- Uncolonizing Our Minds: On the Supreme Court, *Counterpunch*, April 16, 2010

- Law to Criminalize Fracking, August 2011. DRAFT conceived by Sovereign People Action Network (SPAN) of Ulster and Green Counties, New York State

- Richard Grossman on Usurpation and the Corporation as Crime, *Corporate Crime Reporter*, October 6, 2011

- Grossman Says Citizens United, Personhood Fetish, Greed and Corruption Are Diversions, *Corporate Crime Reporter*, October 17, 2011

- Interview with Richard Grossman, *Corporate Crime Reporter*, October 17, 2011

- An Act To Criminalize Chartered, Incorporated Business Entities - a work in progress, October 2011

Other articles online by Richard L. Grossman:

Viewpoint: "Cleaning the Air Gives Way to Protecting Profits," *In These Times*, April 25, 1990
https://www.unz.com/print/ InTheseTimes-1990apr25-00016/

"How Environmental Law Has Failed Us," *Progressive Review*, June 1995, pp. 1-2
https://www.unz.com/print/ ProgressiveRev-1995jun-00001/

"Richard Grossman Interview" by Ruth Conniff,
The Progressive, March 1, 2002
https://progressive.org/ dispatches/richard-grossman-interview-Conniff-020301/

ACKNOWLEDGEMENTS

Thanks go to the 'team' behind this work. Three people who knew and believed in the importance of Richard's work offered the confidence and advice needed to proceed with publication.

Peter Kellman is a longtime labor, civil rights and safe energy activist now involved with wife Rebekah Yonan in the New Agriculture movement in Maine. Richard Grossman's friend and colleague, Pete gave on-going, helpful editorial advice, background information and all-around encouragement.

Researcher and web archivist David Ratcliffe and I met for the first time halfway between our eastern and western Massachusetts homes, and shared enthusiasm for Richard's work. Says Dave: "I met Richard Grossman in 1996 when he and Ward Morehouse gave a presentation on Revoking The Corporation in Palo Alto, California on January 26. The scope and depth of the frame each man expressed was breathtaking. I had never encountered such far-ranging understanding of the history of the corporate form before, and especially, after the American Revolution." Richard agreed to Dave's request to put his many writings online, creating a unique and valuable archive among others featured at *https://ratical.org/corporations/*.

The third in this group I hope to meet one day in person. Maria Gilardin, talented radio journalist in California, made clear, powerful recordings of Richard's talks when he was on the west coast. They are featured in her radio series and archive at *https://tucradio.org/* Maria presents original material that would otherwise have been lost, with clear affection and admiration for the speaker.

As the book neared publication, two former Project on Corporations, Law and Democracy (POCLAD) colleagues were especially helpful: Greg Coleridge for outreach to an interested public, and Mike Ferner for proofreading this version of his old friend's words.

The moment I saw local artist Cynthia Fisher's "Spawning Salmon" mosaic I knew it was the perfect cover for this work. She agreed to its use years before publication, and with good humor awaited the final result.

Our back cover is from another superb artist. Thanks to Rob Shetterly for his many portraits of "Americans Who Tell the Truth," among them both Richard Grossman and Peter Kellman, and for permission to use Richard's image on the back cover.

It took a while to find the right way to get this book out, but with Paul Richmond's Human Error Publishing we found our literary grassroots with a home grown publisher who is himself a skilled and talented artist, and a pleasure to work with.

Last but hardly least, my thanks for the ongoing support of family and friends. Among them Jeanine, John and Jay, who provided space and time in Cape Ann to focus on the work. And to Parker, who kept reminding me of its importance.

About the editor

Anna Gyorgy tries to live an ecological life, while gardening, writing and organizing for change. Active against nuclear power from 1974, she and Richard Grossman met in October 1976 at the antinuclear Clamshell Alliance's safe energy fair. Later, as Director of Public Citizen's Critical Mass Energy Project in Washington, DC, she knew Richard, then leading Environmentalists for Full Employment, as a supportive friend and mentor in the big city. During later decades spent outside the USA, she appreciated his writings and teachings, and they remained friends until his passing. Back in her Western Massachusetts home, she works with the Traprock Center for Peace & Justice, and gardens.